Dino World!

Dinosaur Fossils

by Leonie Bennett

Consultant: Luis M. Chiappe, Ph.D.
Director of the Dinosaur Institute
Natural History Museum of Los Angeles County

BEARPORT
PUBLISHING

NEW YORK, NEW YORK

Credits

Cover, Title Page, 4, 6, 7, 16, 22M, 22B, 23T, 24: Shutterstock; 5: Science Photo Library; 8–9, 21, 23M, 23B: Ticktock Media Archive; 10, 11, 12, 13, 14, 15, 19B: Ian Jackson; 17, 18: Corbis; 19T, 20: Natural History Museum; 22T: Lisa Alderson.

Every effort has been made by ticktock Entertainment Ltd. to trace copyright holders. We apologize in advance for any omissions. We would be pleased to insert the appropriate acknowledgments in any subsequent edition of this publication.

Library of Congress Cataloging-in-Publication Data

Bennett, Leonie.
  Dinosaur fossils / by Leonie Bennett.
      p. cm. — (I love reading. Dino World!)
  Includes bibliographical references and index.
  ISBN-13: 978-1-59716-555-6 (library binding)
  ISBN-10: 1-59716-555-7 (library binding)
  1. Dinosaurs—Juvenile literature. 2. Fossils—Juvenile literature. 3. Paleontologists—Juvenile literature. I. Title.

  QE861.5.B4454 2008
  567.9—dc22

                              2007017657

Copyright © 2007 ticktock Entertainment Ltd.
2 Orchard Business Centre, North Farm Road, Tunbridge Wells, Kent, TN2 3XF, UK
Published in the United States of America by Bearport Publishing Company, Inc.
United States text copyright © 2008 Bearport Publishing Company, Inc.

For more information, write to Bearport Publishing Company, Inc., 101 Fifth Avenue, Suite 6R, New York, New York 10003. Printed in the United States of America.

10 9 8 7 6 5 4 3 2

Contents

What is a fossil?

A fossil is what is left of an animal or plant that lived long ago.

Can you see an animal shape in this stone?

It is a fossil of a *Tyrannosaurus rex*.

fossil

Tyrannosaurus rex
(ti-*ran*-uh-SOR-uhss REKS)

Types of fossils

There are many different types of fossils.

Some fossils are parts of plants.

Others are marks made by plants.

Some fossils are parts of animals.

Others are marks, such as **footprints**, made by animals.

Why are fossils important?

Fossils help us learn about animals that no longer live on Earth.

Parasaurolophus was a dinosaur that lived millions of years ago.

This is a *Parasaurolophus* fossil.

> ***Parasaurolophus***
> (***par*-ah-sor-AH-loh-fuhss)**

9

Becoming a fossil

Hypsilophodon was a small dinosaur that ate plants.

This *Hypsilophodon* died millions of years ago.

Hypsilophodon
(hip-sih-LOH-fuh-don)

It fell into a lake and drowned.

11

At the bottom of a lake

Hypsilophodon lay on the bottom of the lake.

Animals ate all of its skin and flesh.

At last, only its bones were left.

Finally, a fossil!

Soon mud and sand covered its bones.

Millions of years went by.

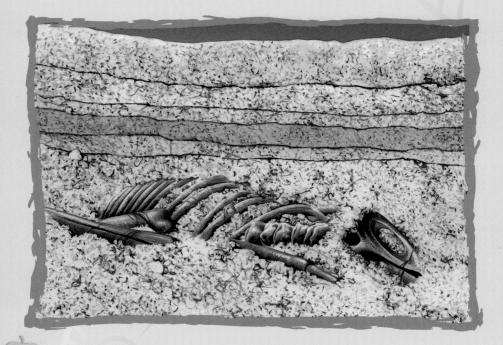

Minerals from the water helped turn the bones to stone.

This *Hypsilophodon* was now a fossil.

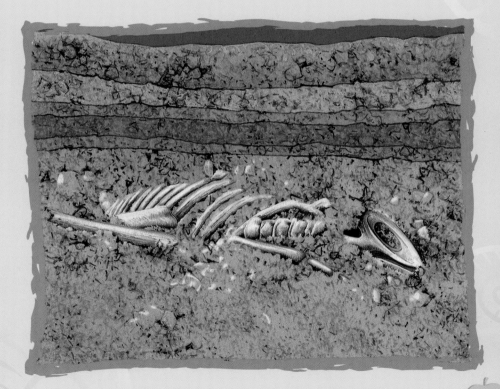

Finding a fossil

After millions of years, the lake dried up.

Now, part of the fossil could be seen.

A young girl and her dad were the first to find it.

They told some **scientists**.

The scientists came and dug up all the fossil bones in the area.

It's *Hypsilophodon*!

The scientists wanted to find out what the dinosaur looked like.

They put the bones together.

The animal's **skeleton** was placed in a museum.

Now, many people can see *Hypsilophodon*.

More fossils

This is an ichthyosaur fossil.

The name means "fish-lizard."

**ichthyosaur
(IK-thee-oh-*sor*)**

This fossil is the **skull** of *Stygimoloch*.

It is also called a **bonehead**.

Stygimoloch
(stij-ee-MOLL-ok)

Glossary

bonehead (BOHN-hed)
a type of dinosaur that
had a dome-like skull

footprints (FUT-prints)
marks made by feet

minerals (MIN-ur-uhlz)
substances found in
nature that are not
plants or animals

22

scientists (SYE-uhn-tists)
people who study nature

skeleton (SKEL-uh-tuhn)
the framework of bones
that protect or support
the body

skull (SKUHL)
the part of the
skeleton that is
inside the head

23

Index

Read More

Baily, Jacqui. *Monster Bones: The Story of a Dinosaur Fossil.* Minneapolis, MN: Picture Window Books (2004).

Nye, Bill. *Bill Nye the Science Guy's Great Big Dinosaur Dig.* New York: Hyperion (2002).

Learn More Online

To learn more about the world of dinosaurs, visit
www.bearportpublishing.com/ILoveReading